From CAMPUS TO CORPORATE

Soft Skills and Etiquette Tips to Transition with Confidence

MARLA HARR

ISBN: 978-0-9863638-0-1

First Printing, June 2015

Second Printing, April 2025

Published by Business Etiquette International, Phoenix, AZ 85016

Illustrations by: Azalea Patricia
www.AzaleaPatricia.weebly.com

Dedication

This book is dedicated to my mom and dad, Joe and Anne. They worked so hard and were so proud to have put four children through college. They were always there to encourage and support us through school and our transition into the working world.

Thank you for the strong work ethic and drive to succeed that you have given me.

All my love,

Marla

Table of Contents

FOREWORD

There are oftentimes we don't see the forest for the trees. I believe this tried and true saying epitomizes the knowledge that Ms. Harr imparts in *From Campus to Corporate.* Many of us take communication and working with others as a given. The workplace has polices; we have been trained socially and culturally, and, *of course,* we apply all of this knowledge in our day-to-day work practices. Right? Unfortunately, this is not the case.

Being a diverse community, we are raised in different cultures. Many students and new employees have not worked in a formal corporate environment. They are not aware of the importance of personal interactions in the workplace and/or the role they should play. Students move from an environment of "all about me" to one of "all about the team." This can be a difficult transition.

We just have to look around to see the dramatic change in social interactions in any environment. People are on their cell phones in the car, at work, during dinner, at a concert, in a park . . . you name it. They are engaged with the device, not engaged in social interactions with those around them. So what does that mean? It means that many of us are no longer aware of our environment. We are not paying attention to our fellow worker; we are not observing acceptable and non-acceptable business practices; nor are we exhibiting the behaviors that are necessary to be effective in the workplace.

From my perspective, this book helps those individuals graduating from school or those who are re-entering the workforce to ensure they have the skills and can apply them to be effective and successful. As a mother of two college-age students, I experience these behaviors first hand. I get texts from my children who are only a room away. Instead of setting up a meeting with a college professor to discuss a problem, they send an email. The practice of face-to-face discussion is becoming a lost art, which impacts teamwork and effective communication between co-workers. *From Campus to Corporate* identifies necessary practices, the 5 C's of

interpersonal skills and your personal responsibilities in the workplace.

This book increases the reader's awareness
of issues that impact others. Ms. Harr pro-
vides simple ways to interact more smoothly
in the work environment, ensuring your ability to move forward with poise and confidence. We all want to be respected and held
in high esteem. *From Campus to Corporate*
not only teaches you how to achieve this for
yourself, but more importantly, how to give
it to others. Definitely recommended reading for anyone who is serious about themselves and their careers.

MaryAnn Guerra, MBA
Chief Executive Officer
Aesthetics Biomedical

ACKNOWLEDGMENTS

Anyone writing a book for the first time can tell you there are more challenges than you think, and many times when the words are just not there. This book was written with the help and support of my siblings Michael, Diana, MaryAnn, and my nephew Bryan.

To my wonderful friend Grey, who taught me a lot about writing and listening when the words would not come, my editor Caren for her patience and expertise, my Master Mind group who always supported me, and my California ladies who cheered me on.

To The Protocol School of Washington® and Pamela Eyring, whose training has been essential to my understanding of proper business etiquette and international protocols.

And especially to my amazingly supportive partner, Mack Jones, without whose love and encouragement this book would never have been done.

Then to all of you, too many to mention, who had a positive and enriching impact on my business career, especially my mentors, who made me look good.

INTRODUCTION

If I knew then what I know now, as the old saying goes, how much easier the start of my career would have been after graduating college. Remembering the uncertainty, struggle, and occasional tears, I wrote this book to help make the transition from college and the entry into management easier for others. If you are willing to make the few changes required for today's business world, this book will help you move through your entire career with confidence, skill, and know-how.

During my time as a human resource manager and trainer, I became the mentor, coach, and cheerleader for new executive hires. With their recent degree in hand, or their knowledge learned through moving up within the company, they understood the new job responsibilities expected of them, but they weren't prepared at all for the intense demands of corporate culture and relationship building; what I call *the soft skills*.

As an instructor at Arizona State University and California State University, it is clear to me that even today our higher-level educational institutions are great at teaching the technical side of job responsibilities, but ignore the importance of the soft skills required to be successful in a highly competitive global market. People continue to enter the workforce unprepared.

The good news is today's college recruits and entry level managers are technology-driven, career-oriented, and eager to learn. The not so good news is they are generally socially inadequate in business etiquette and the fundamentals of office life. Lacking in these soft skills might be their biggest challenge in advancing their careers.

So, what are soft skills exactly? I break them into two categories: interpersonal skills and personal responsibility.

Interpersonal skills can be remembered as the five C's of soft skills: communication, connection, critical thinking, collaboration, and creativity.

Communication is the most dynamic soft skill, comprising several types, each with many levels. Verbal is face-to-face or a voice message. Written is an email, text, or formal letter. Documentation is manuals, presentation material, or work notes. Non-verbal is our body language that includes facial expressions, posture and even arm movements.

Connection is the ability to build relationships with others. "Others" is defined as your peers, supervisors, other department personnel, and outside resources. It also includes connecting with those of other generations.

Critical thinking is an individual's method of reasoning. It involves being focused, controlled, and having the ability to analyze the information or situation. For example, taking an exam and being part of a team project are two very different critical thinking situations.

Collaboration is two or more individuals working on a common goal or project. It includes the ability to share ideas and to come to consensus as a group. This requires communication, problem-solving, and being group/goal-focused instead of self-focused.

Creativity at work is, in part, motivation, knowledge of the field, and thinking skills. It requires self-confidence, energy, and readiness to share ideas that might be outside the norm.

Personal responsibility soft skills are self-motivation, punctuality, flexibility, and appearance.

Self-motivation is the desire to excel at work. According to Dictionary.com, self-motivation is "the initiative to undertake or continue a task or activity without another's prodding or supervision."

Appearance is to be nicely groomed and appropriately dressed at all times.

Punctuality is to be on time and prepared. It's also keeping commitments to deadlines. It means understanding what the impact of being late has on others and the project.

Flexibility is to be open-minded and willing to make changes.

This may read like an overwhelming and discouraging list of behaviors and skills to learn. However, with the motivation to learn and the willingness to change, the transition to the workplace can be easily accomplished. Taking it step-by-step, these new ways of thinking and behaving will soon become second nature to you.

I have designed this book to be a quick reference manual for individuals. It can also be used as a tool for supervisors and management in the development and training of soft skills as part of their company's orientation programs. Human Resources may find value in the creation of a mentor program, with this book as a guide, to aid in the career progress and retention of future executives.

To your success!

Marla Harr

PHYSICAL POWER POINTS

We are constantly communicating from the moment we wake up to the moment we lay our heads on our pillow at the end of the day. We speak through our writing, be it email, text, or a formal letter. We speak with our voices in face-to-face conversations, voice messages, or on the phone. We speak with our physical body, i.e. our eyes, forehead, and facial expression, our handshake, posture, and our dress. It's important to realize that when we are awake, we are always communicating and sending out messages.

As I stated in the introduction, changing roles from college student to new employee in today's business world requires you to make many behavior and skill changes to ensure a successful career. In this chapter, we are going to look at six power points that send out both physical and non-physical messages.

"The face is a picture of the mind as the eyes are its interpreter." Cicero (106-43 B.C.)

<u>Number 1 – The Eyes Have It</u>

Our eyes convey important unspoken messages. They show if you are listening to the person with whom you are in a conversation. They:

- Show how interested you are in the conversation.

- Tell the other person a bit about your personality.

Eye contact is important in business and vital if you are to present yourself with confidence and poise. You need to know and understand the signals you are sending with your eyes and, equally important; you need to be aware of the eye signals of others.

Our true feelings are expressed primarily in the upper face, through the eyes, brows, and forehead. This is the "business" eye contact zone.

Eye Signals - Business

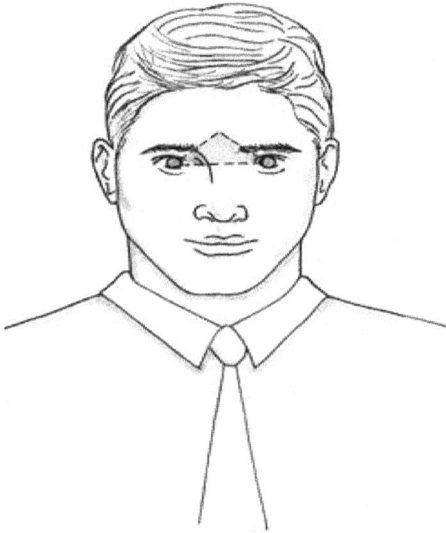

Notice the triangle is centered on the eyes, eyebrows, and forehead. Studies show that true feelings and emotions are expressed mainly in the upper part of your face. Keeping your gaze mainly in this triangle, does several things:

A. Tells the other person you're listening and actually makes you a better listener.
B. Helps you to be aware of the signals the other person is sending, as well as your own.

C. Helps you to focus attention on the person you're talking to and makes them feel important while you look self-confident.
D. Creates a more business like impression.

What do your eyes reveal?

Eye Signals - Social

A gaze below the eye level suggests a social atmosphere is developing. Become aware of the location of your own gaze, as it is not professional. Some people may be uncomfortable if they think you are staring at their nose, mouth, or chin, particularly if they are not happy with these parts of their face.

In business, a good rule to follow is to keep direct eye contact at 40 to 60 percent while engaged in conversation. There are two important points about direct eye contact:

First – When used less than 40-60 percent, you may appear to be shy, shifty, like you are hiding something, or lacking in self-confidence.

Think about a time when you were in a conversation and the person constantly kept looking around; at the door, at other people, out the window, etc. How did that make you feel? I'm betting a bit uncomfortable and that you and the conversation were not important.

Second - If you hold your gaze too long (more than 60%) you may make the person feel they are on the spot, that you're being condescending or even intimidating.

Again, how do you feel when someone is keeping their focus on you and not adjusting their direct eye contact? It's an unnerving and uncomfortable feeling.

When you are talking, watch your listener's eyes to see if you are holding their attention. If the person you're talking to isn't listening, it doesn't matter what you are saying!

> **Biz Tip:** Keep your eyes in the business area [eyes, brows, forehead] 40-60 percent of the conversation time.

Remember, as you transition from the campus atmosphere to the world of the workplace, your relationships are now professional and not the casual friendships you were used to forming. This also holds true if you're making an upward career move from hourly employee to management. Understanding the power of your eye contact can help boost your self-confidence, professional image, and career success.

Number 2 – Step into the Spotlight

The type of entrance you make in attending any business function is so important. In fact, it's vital if you are to present yourself with confidence and poise.

You might be asking yourself, "Why?" That's a great question with a very simple answer. Most people watch the entrance to a room, any room, a conference room, a networking event in a hotel meeting room, or a restaurant. I think you get the picture.

Good news – this is a wonderful window of opportunity for you to make a positive impression. You may have heard it only takes five seconds to make an impression! That's an intimidating statistic, but well researched and documented. Keep in mind we all do this; it's part of being human.

So, the question you need to ask is, "What type of impression do I make when I enter a room?"

What makes a great business entrance? Posture! It instantly creates the impression of a confident, capable person.

    A. Walk in with your head up, spine straight, and shoulders down and relaxed. You will look confident, self-assured, and in control.

    B. Walk in all stooped shoulders and looking down and you'll come across as shy, lacking self-confidence, have low self-esteem, or convey that you are uncomfortable.

    C. Walk in with quite the strut and you can come across as arrogant, overly confident, and maybe someone others don't want to meet.

Good Posture   Poor Posture

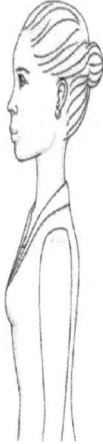 

Biz Tip: 5 second rule – you have 5 seconds to make a first impression – make it a good one!

Now that you have the posture down, what's next? A few more tips to aid you in looking confident:

- Walk through the doorway and move to the right if right-handed or left if you are left-handed.
  - Never stop in the door where you are blocking the entrance.

> Someone may be behind you. You don't want anyone to run into you! That would not be the most graceful entrance.

- Pause.
    - Gives you the chance to spot key people, find a chair, or someone you know. You can head to a seat or a conversation with confidence.
    - It allows people to see you before you mingle with others.
- Always dress appropriately for the function you are attending. Dress is as important as posture in the 5 second impression you are creating for yourself. If you are not sure what dress is appropriate, ask the person who is putting on the meeting or event.

Biz Tip: Proper posture is the key. It instantly creates the sense of a confident person.

<u>Number 3 – Handling the Handshake</u>

Ever wonder where the ritual of handshaking began?

"The ritual of shaking hands arose sometime during the Roman Empire, not out of courtesy and good will, but out of fear. The human past was one of danger, where wild beasts and bandits roamed and men walked around well-armed. Strangers immediately aroused suspicion...

In order to become friends, you first had to make sure the other man would not attack. You either laid down your weapons or kept your right (dominant) hands away from them, displaying empty palms. (Left-handedness was considered evil in those days, so you exposed right hands.) To be certain, neither of you would grab his sword and lunge. You grasped right hands. Thus, the handshake was born – not of friendship but of mistrust."

Robert E. Brown and Dorothea Johnson, *The Power of Handshaking*

Today, the western handshake has become a universal, non-verbal form of greeting and communication. A handshake reveals many things about you or the person with whom you are shaking hands. It can show personality, feelings, motivation, and attitude toward others. In essence a handshake is communication that doesn't require an explanation and is not often misunderstood.

You are judged by your handshake and you make judgments about others when you shake their hand.

> **Biz Tip:** When conducting international business learn the proper handshake or greeting for that country. This is a positive and appropriate gesture in building relationships.

Let's get to the steps that ensure a commanding handshake:

1. Right hand – should always be free, ready to shake hands.
2. Left hand – hold only one item; you don't want to be fumbling with items if you need your right hand free to shake hands.
3. Extend hand thumb up and fingers out. This allows the other person's hand to connect with yours for a genuine handshake.

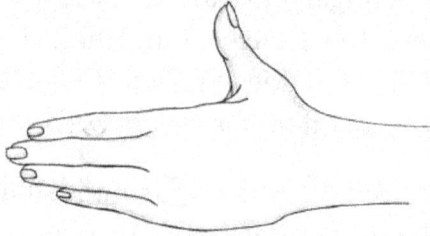

4. Connect hands – web-to-web – this is the area between your thumb and index finger.
5. Shake from the elbow – not the wrist or shoulder.
6. Two smooth pumps – then release hands.

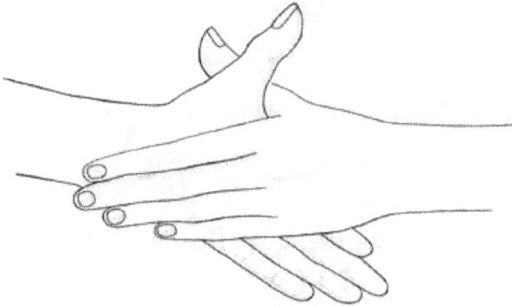

A few extra tips:

- Stand facing the individual with your shoulders squared to theirs. This allows you to see the person's face and name badge. Be sure to look them in the eye, smile and call them by name. Use titles if appropriate.

- Name badge – goes on your right shoulder so people can easily see your name as they're shaking your hand. Most people tend to place the badge on the left shoulder, or with men, on the breast pocket of their suit. This is incorrect.

- Avoid thumb down, fingers curled – this does not allow for a solid grasp.

- Clammy hands control – spray/rub clear antiperspirant on your palms.

- Avoid fragrance – use it sparingly, many people are allergic to fragrance.

- Avoid large rings – they can interfere with the proper grip and can be painful if your hand is squeezed too hard.

- Awareness alert – be attentive to others with a disability.

- In the United States, there is no set rule for who offers a hand first. The person who extends their hand first benefits as this establishes that you are comfortable taking the initiative, are not timid and have self-confidence – all pluses in making a good impression.

- A woman who extends her hand first removes any hesitation a man might have in offering his hand.

> **Biz Tip:** Handshaking rule – gender doesn't matter in western business; both men and women use the same handshake.

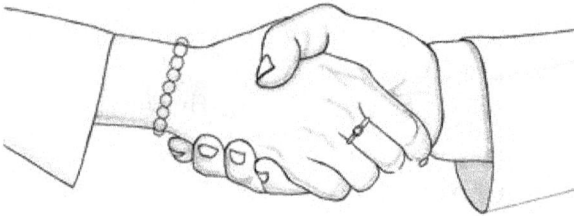

You shake hands when:

- Someone comes into your office or home.
- You meet someone outside your office or home.
- You enter a room and are greeted by those you know or are introduced to someone you don't know.
- Leave a gathering or say goodbye to an individual.
- Congratulating someone who won an award or gave a speech.
- Consoling someone.
- Concluding a business transaction or contract.

Handshaking Internationally

- Know the correct greeting for that nation before you go.
- The Western handshake is accepted throughout the world in business today. As relationships are built, be aware the formal western handshake may be replaced with a culture's accepted greeting. For example, in the Middle East (Arab) when men are conducting business the custom is for men to embrace and kiss on both cheeks. Men do not shake hands with women in the Middle East.
- Outside the United States, international protocol is that you shake hands with everyone in a group. Don't stop halfway with a "hello everyone" wave to the rest of the people. This is deemed a rejection by those you omitted and everyone notices.
- Shake hands when you arrive and depart. Your grip should be firm, never hard; it may be lighter in some cultures.
- Stay away from the fingertip handshake; it's unpopular around the world.
- In some cultures, women in business do not touch a man, so a

handshake is unacceptable. Know this before you go and just give a simple smile and verbal greeting.

Number 4 – First Class Introductions

We make ourselves known by how we introduce ourselves and others. Often it's difficult to go up and meet new people or a company executive. The thing to remember is you are not alone! Many new and recently promoted employees are unsure of the correct etiquette and protocol, so the natural instinct is to delay or wait for someone else to step in and make the introductions. Good news – learning how to do a "first class" introduction is an easy behavior skill to master and incorporate into your everyday actions.

What to say when introducing yourself to generate a first-class image:

"Hi." is defiantly not enough.

"Hello." is a better word, but again, not enough in business.

"Hello, I'm Nancy Smith." better but not quite there yet.

"Hello, I'm Nancy Smith, with the ABC Company." almost there.

"Hello, I'm Nancy Smith, Sales Director with the ABC Company." This is a great self-introduction!

Why? Because Nancy has given her full name, what her position is (helps others to understand her role and responsibilities) and the company she represents. In business, this is the type of information you need to start a conversation and establish connections.

Take Accountability and Introduce Yourself When:

- You recognize someone and they don't recognize you – always put the other person at ease and mention where you previously met.
- Attend any meeting, networking, or business function.
- You are seated next to a stranger. Don't wait for them, be polite and introduce yourself. This will break the ice and help start the conversation.
- The person introducing you forgets your name – help them out and say your name. We have all, at some time, forgotten a person's name. We know how uncomfortable that can be.

> **Biz Tip:** Introduce yourself – it's your responsibility and the professional thing to do.

When another has introduced you to someone new, your response can say a lot about you. Responding to Introductions:

- "Hello." Sounds too immature for business.
- "Hello, it's a pleasure to meet you, Mr. Jones." Excellent! Using the person's name helps you to remember their name.

When the person who introduced you did not use your title or company name, be sure to include it in your response. By repeating your name, title, and company it helps to reinforce it for Mr. Jones.

Protocol for Business Introductions:

- Who will be introduced to whom is determined by their rank or position within the organization. The person who holds the highest position takes priority over others who work there.
- Elected officials and the military also have rank and position status.

Formula for Introductions

- Higher Position; i.e. *President, Vice President, Director, etc.* RECEIVES Lower Position; i.e. *manger, sales person, new associate.* By RECEIVE I mean the lower-level position person is introduced "to" the higher level person.

Order of Introductions

- Junior executive or associate is introduced to the Senior executive. Non-official person is introduced to the elected official person.
- Company executive or associate is introduced to the Client.

Note: Company executives being introduced to the client seems strange to some people. The rule is simple – without clients you would not have a business. Clients take precedence!

For an easy way to remember how to introduce someone, it's useful to think of two music images. One is the "Happy Birthday" song, and the other is the rock group "U2."

Correct is The Happy Birthday Song – think happy birthday **"to you."**
Incorrect is the Rock group U2 – think **"you to."**

For example, Mary is going to introduce her new employee John Smith to the president of the company, Mr. Anderson.

Incorrect: "Mr. Anderson, I would like <u>you to</u> meet John Smith, our new employee in accounting."

Correct: "Mr. Anderson, I would like to introduce <u>to you</u> John Smith, our new employee in accounting."

Biz Tip: A higher level executive receives a lower level employee.

Hints and Tips:
- Unnecessary gestures – keep hands low, don't pull people together.
- Look at each person.
- You are introduced in error – correct immediately in a positive tone of voice.
- Your firm is misidentified – correct immediately in a positive tone of voice.

- Always stand – the only two exceptions are a disability or the position of your seat makes it difficult to stand.

Networking Event A Few More Tips:
- Eat a small amount of food before you go.
- Key persons – know who you should meet and who can introduce you.
- Peers – make yourself known to those you do know.
- Join a conversation – skillfully join in a conversation. A networking event is designed for people to meet new people, so don't be shy about entering a group of attendees. Catch the eye of one of the group members and simply ask if you can join. "Do you mind if I join your group?" Chances are they will respond with something like, "please do." Be sure to introduce yourself properly with your name, position, and company.
- Shake hands – with everyone in a group.

Number 5 – Do Sweat the Small Talk

There is an interesting study from Harvard University, The Carnegie Foundation, and Stanford Research Institute. They found that

85% of your job success is based on your people or "soft" skills and not your technical knowledge of your job responsibilities. Soft skills are your ability to get along and work well with others.

Your people skills determine if you:
- Will, or will not get a job.
- Be retained or let go from a job.
- Passed over or given the promotion.

> **Biz Tip:** Our people skills are the prime qualities that make and keep us employed.

Let's talk small talk. It's an important people skill because it:
- Breaks the ice – helps to make others more comfortable.
- Establishes a connection – helps to build relationships
- Doesn't require original or profound conversation – it's "chit-chat."
- Is the polite thing to do – it's part of showing good manners.

In order to excel at small talk, you need to:

- Be well-informed – keep up with what is going on locally, nationally, and internationally.
- Focus on the other person – ask open-ended questions, learn about them.
- Don't interrupt – sometimes this is hard to do but always allow a person to complete their thought.
- Listen – keep your focus on the other person and what they are saying.
- Think before you speak – once you say something, you can't take it back.
- Close a conversation – always end the conversation. Example: "It's been a pleasure talking with you Mary," or "Mary, I look forward to talking with you next week."

There are certain subjects that are best to stay clear of:
- Political issues
- Religion
- Your health or diet habits
- Costs of things
- Personal questions – For example: asking if someone is still married or is the divorce final, asking how much they paid for their house or car, etc.
- Mean gossip
- Off-color jokes

- Any issue that could be considered controversial

Number 6 – How to Really Use Your Business Card

How you present and use your business card is an important part in building professional relationships. Your card represents you and is part of your company branding. It should be given to someone in such a way that it is remembered and kept instead of tossed as soon as you turn your back.

Follow these first-class business card etiquette Dos and Don'ts.

Dos for Business Card Etiquette

1. Present the card with the print facing the recipient so they will not have to turn it around to read it.
2. When receiving a card, take the time to look at it. A card is representative of the person and doing so shows respect.
3. Pay attention to the conversation; and write pertinent notes on the card later.
4. Carry cards in a card case to keep them fresh and protected.

5. Before attending an event, always put a supply of cards in your suit pocket for easy access. Keep them in the right pocket and place cards you receive in the left pocket. You don't want to get your card mixed up with those you have accepted.

6. Present your business card to the receptionist each time you visit a company. It helps the receptionist announce you.

7. Carry business cards at social events in case a good business contact presents itself. However, be discreet if cards are exchanged, especially in a private home.

Don'ts for Business Card Etiquette

1. Don't give out a business card that is defective, out of date, or soiled.

2. Don't pass out your cards like flyers. You will appear pushy and unprofessional if you are handing your card out indiscriminately.

3. Don't force your card on anyone.

4. Don't offer your card early in a conversation. Wait to see if there is a good business connection first.

5. Junior executives in the same firm don't give or request cards from senior executives. Allow the senior executive to request your card or offer theirs.

6. Don't leave a person's card on the table. Take the card with you and dispose of it at your home or office if you're not interested.

Biz Tip: Your business card is an important part of your marketing materials, keep them pristine.

The Modern Business Card Exchange

Technology has significantly changed the way professionals exchange contact information. While traditional paper business cards are still used, many people now prefer digital alternatives that are more efficient, sustainable, and integrated with their workflow. Here are a few ways technology has transformed this exchange:

1. **Digital Business Cards** Platforms like HiHello, Blinq, and Beaconstac let professionals create and share digital business cards via QR codes,

links, or NFC (Near Field Communication). These cards can be updated in real time, ensuring that contact details remain accurate.

2. **QR Code Integration** Many professionals now include a QR code on their traditional business card, which leads directly to a LinkedIn profile, company website, or digital contact card. This makes it easy for someone to scan and save information instantly.

3. **Near Field Communication Cards (NFC)** NFC-enabled business cards allow you to share your details with just a tap on a smartphone, making the exchange seamless and more interactive.

4. **Social Media and Professional Platforms** LinkedIn has become a go-to tool for exchanging contact information. Features like LinkedIn's "Find Nearby" function allow professionals to instantly connect without exchanging physical cards.

5. **Email Signatures and Virtual Cards** Many professionals include their contact details, LinkedIn profile,

or a digital card link in their email signature, making every email an opportunity to share contact information.

6. **Networking Apps and CRM Integration** Apps like CamCard and Evernote Scannable allow users to scan and store business cards digitally, linking them to CRM tools for better follow-up and relationship management.

7. **Customizable Contact Pages** Services like Linktree and About.me enable professionals to create a digital hub with links to their social media, portfolios, and contact details, offering a more dynamic alternative to traditional cards.

Best Practices for a Professional Exchange

Make It Personal – Introduce yourself before sharing your contact information. A personal touch makes it more memorable.

Follow Up Within 48 Hours – Send a quick message or LinkedIn request to solidify the connection.

Be Selective – Don't hand out cards to everyone; focus on meaningful networking.

Keep Your Info Up to Date – Ensure your contact details and digital profiles are always current.

Despite these advancements, the etiquette of exchanging contact information remains essential. Whether handing out a physical card or sharing a digital one, making a personal connection and following up after the exchange is what ensures that your contact information is valued and remembered.

Biz Tip: Always have a backup method. If someone prefers a physical card, keep a few on hand!

Chapter in Review

Six important areas were covered: eye contact, the entrance, the handshake, proper introductions, small talk and the business card. These will help you create a professional image of confidence and control. You can master these with practice and a commitment to being a truly polished professional.

CONQUER THE CORPORATE CLOSET

"You never have a second chance to make a good first impression."
John T Molloy, Author of *Dress for Success*

In 1961, Mr. Molloy became the first person to actively promote how you dress with how successful you become. His advice of suits and ties for men and skirted suits for women became the dressing "bible" for corporate America for almost 30 years.

Then the dot.com boom hit and suddenly wearing khakis was a career move. As the tech industry took off, white shirts and ties were replaced by polos and tees. Trousers became jeans or, sometimes shorts. Everyone was trying to entice the Gen Y workforce.

The bubble burst in 2001 and since that time corporations have been moving steadily back toward a more traditional look. Even with "Casual Friday" or a "business casual" workplace, you are still judged by how you look.

No matter how good you are at your job, how you dress can affect career advancement.

The Interview

Few things in life are more stressful than your first interviews. Competition is fierce. It's not always the best-qualified candidate that gets the job. You also have to sell yourself. In the case of the interview, you are the brand and your appearance is your logo.

First impressions are based on what we see, not what we hear. Most professionals form their idea of how well you will do on the job, from your clothes and grooming. So put some effort into making sure you are projecting the right first impression.

This will hold true even if you are already an employee and are simply interviewing for a higher-level position within the organization. If you come to the interview dressed as you would for your current job, the impression you may be giving is that you are not serious about advancement – that you don't have the savvy to move to the next level.

Here are some things you should do to prepare for your interview so you will know how to dress:

- Contact Human Resources and ask about the dress code.
- Find out who you will be interviewing with and their level within the organization.
- If you know someone at the company, call them to get their take on appropriate dress.
- Go to the office, specifically around lunch, so you can see many people coming and going. How are they dressed? Can you tell management from staff?
- Look at their website – how do they project their employees?

Biz Tip: The goal is to look the part. You need to look like the sort of person the company would want to employ and the sort who values themselves and their career.

Once you understand the appropriate dress, the next step is to plan what you will wear. You want to be comfortable and confident in whatever you choose, so don't wait until the last minute to decide. Some guidelines to keep in mind:

- Be sure your attire is appropriate for the season, industry, or culture.
- Wear clothes that fit not too loose or too tight; get alterations if necessary.
- Everything needs to be cleaned and pressed.
- Don't look dated. This will brand you as conservative and unimaginative.
- Keep jewelry to a minimum.
- Make sure your shoes are polished and not worn.
- If in a "business casual" company, make sure to dress to the higher end. More on this later.
- Carry a quality leather folder and pen; women, your purse should also be of good quality and not over-stuffed.
- Grooming must be impeccable. I've devoted an entire section to grooming.

Biz Tip: The interview is not a time to make a fashion statement. Prep your outfit ahead of time to make the best first impression possible.

I'm Hired, Now What?

Some very good advice I've taken to heart over the years is that you should always dress for the job you want – not for the job you have. So, unless you're in a position that requires a uniform, you'll want to see how your boss, or your boss's boss, dresses and try to emulate them.

Remember, people form impressions about your work and your performance as much by how you dress as what you say or do. An administrative assistant who wears a suit or jacket and skirt to work every day is much more likely to be seen as promotable as one who comes to work in pants and an open blouse.

That doesn't mean you have to become a clone. You can, and you should, allow your own personality and flair to come through. It's easiest to do this with ties for men and with blouse choices for women.

Dressing For Men

- Short-sleeved shirts with ties are never appropriate unless you are an airline pilot. you'll look school-boyish. Even without ties, they never look as professional as long-sleeved shirts.
- Ties should reach the top of your belt.
- Your belt should match the color of your shoes and so should your socks.

- In terms of suits, navy promotes authority and gray more approachable. But not light gray – it will never look expensive.
- If your trousers have belt loops, then wear a belt, not suspenders.
- Shoes should be thin-soled, lace-ups with a suit.

Dressing For Women

- Matching suits are no longer necessary to project a professional appearance but they are still required under some circumstances. Know your environment.
- Since women's styles change frequently, your shoes should be updated every six months. Heels no higher than 2 to 2 ½ inches and color should be no lighter than your hemline.
- Skirts should be knee length.
- Express your personality through the blouses you match with your suits, but always avoid loud prints.
- If nylons are required, make sure they are free of snags and runs.
- Navy, black, and gray can be worn year-round.

Biz Tip: Buy the most expensive clothes and accessories you can afford. Do not overlook your shoes – they are one of the first items to be judged.

Casual Attire and Corporate Events

There is so much confusion over "casual" attire in the workplace. Companies don't put much effort into defining what casual means to them, ignoring the fact that their customers are forming opinions of their "brand" by what their employees wear.

Casual does not mean you get to wear to work what you might wear on the weekends. It is never, ever your favorite pair of jeans with the knees ripped out or sweatpants of any kind.

Casual is putting together a wardrobe that maintains the respect and credibility you deserve.

- Don't mix your looks, i.e. wearing a quality belt with casual shoes.
- A jacket always empowers a look but don't wear your suit jacket. Get a quality single-breasted sports jacket.
- Never leave your shirt untucked and make sure it is pressed.

- Avoid t-shirts, particularly those with logos.
- No sneakers.
- No strappy tops/dresses for women – minimize the amount of skin.

Biz Tip: Regardless of casual dress, you should always keep a suit handy in your office for last minute meetings with clients who would expect it.

Dressing professionally is required when attending corporate events. No matter the location or the circumstance, your goal is always to be perceived as capable, credible, and confident.

For example, if the company is having a cookout around a pool, appropriate attire might be knee-length shorts and a t-shirt, but it would not be a bathing suit. Even if you have the perfect body, this is not the image you want coming to your boss's mind every time he sees you.

Clean and Crisp

Now that you understand how to dress, let's talk about how to groom. Whether you appear clean and fresh says a lot about the respect you have for others. Things like bad breath, smoking odors, and un-fresh clothes (body odor) will turn people off and keep you from putting your best foot forward. The impression you'll leave is "if he/she doesn't care about personal hygiene, how much do they care about their work?"

So here are some things to think about before you leave the house:

- Hair should be clean and styled. If your hair is long (men and women) it should be tied back or kept under control.
- Fragrances should be avoided but if you must use them, do not let them be overpowering.
- Nails should be clean and well-manicured. They are seen constantly. Use light polish only.
- Makeup should be light and professional.
- Mustaches and beards are still off-putting in some industries. If you can't live without them, make sure they are neatly trimmed.
- Use deodorant.
- Keep a toothbrush and toothpaste at the office.

- Men – keep an electric razor for that 5 o'clock shadow.
- Women – keep extra nylons at work.

> **Biz Tip:** Look in the mirror before you leave for work. Is your appearance sending the right message?

Chapter in Review

Do your homework before going to a job interview. How does the company dress?

Always keep your look professional. Dress for the job you want to have. Show your employers you value yourself as well as the company.

Buy the most expensive clothes and accessories you can afford. Don't mix your looks; quality suit with bargain basement shoes.

Personal hygiene matters – it shows respect for others and for your job. Don't let sloppiness in your appearance reflect on your work.

3 CS OF CUBICLE CONDUCT

"Corporations no longer try to fit square pegs into round holes; they just fit them into square cubicles."
Robert Brault, American Writer

Having spent many years of my professional life working in a cubicle, I understand the work environment and challenges of cubicle life. When I first started working for a major corporation as a training manager, all executives had an office. Along came a design efficiency consultant and the next thing we knew, we were giving up our office with a door and moving into the more efficient, cost-saving world of the open cubicle. It was a perk if you were at a high enough level to get the tall walls. Gone were the doors, the privacy, and the quiet and comfort of having a private workspace.

Today, most employees are used to having a cubicle for their workspace. The challenge is individuals forget their space is really a part of other people's space as well. This brings us to "Cubicle Etiquette." It starts with each person having an expanded awareness of the surrounding space. Our behavior affects the employees who share this common space. When we pay attention to how we use this space, we show respect and consideration to others. These are the building blocks for strong business relationships and teams.

Follow these three cubicle conduct "house rules" and help create a harmonious and productive workplace:

Rule 1 – Courtesy
"Rudeness is the weak man's imitation of strength."   Eric Hoffer, American Writer

Cubicle courtesy starts with each person having an awareness of the surrounding space, which is larger than just their cubicle. Remember, your behavior affects all the employees who share a common space. Be kind, courteous, and respectful at all times.

- Respect a person's time. Since there is no door to close, your co-worker can't easily signal they are busy.
- As a visitor, "knock" lightly or say, "May I come in?"
- Do not assume the person is automatically available to talk with you.

Ask if it is a good time to talk. If not, ask when they will be available.

- Don't barge into a cubicle. This is someone's office, even though it does not have a door.
- No hovering at or over a cubicle if the person is on the phone. Leave and come back later.
- Never use profanity in the workplace. It is unprofessional and you don't know who it may offend.
- Avoid personal calls. No one appreciates having to listen to them.

Biz Tip: People use closed doors to indicate they're busy. Cubicles have no doors. Respect a person's time.

Rule 2 – Clutter and Workspace Décor

Creating a space that is reflective of your personality and style is important to your comfort and productivity at work. However, you need to keep in mind your job and your work environment. Do you meet face-to-face with clients where the company image is important? Is your company culture conservative, such as a bank, or is it creative, as in a marketing or design company? Know the expectations of your company's image and standards for its employees. If you are not sure, ask your boss or just look around!

How you behave and personalize your workspace shows anyone who walks by your level of professionalism. Always put your best image forward. Keep these few points in mind as you create your professional workspace.

- Don't pin-up anything distasteful: pictures, jokes, quotes, etc.
- Keep away from risqué, gross, obscene, racist, sexist, political, or religious overtones.
- Never pin-up anything that would be thought "anti-corporate," like an article from a newspaper or magazine.
- Keep your workspace clean and professional looking. Request the supplies you need to maintain order with your paperwork and projects.

Biz Tip: How you behave and personalize your workspace shows anyone who walks by your level of professionalism.

Rule 3 – Chat Time

"Good neighbors keep their noise to themselves."
Les Blomberg, Executive Director,
Noise Pollution Clearinghouse

We sometime forget that noise control (sounds like a loud voice, music, laughing) is part of having good manners and workplace courtesy. Excessive sound can be stressful, frustrating and, in some cases even painful to fellow employees. Show your respect and politeness to others by keeping your noise levels down.

- Be respectful of "noise." If you have a loud voice, get in the habit of speaking more softly.
- If your company allows music at your desk, keep it low or use head-phones.
- Ask fellow employees to "quiet down" if needed; do it politely, without anger and with a smile.
- If a discussion is confidential or private, find a conference room or office for the call or meeting.
- If you plan to use a speakerphone, find a conference room or private office for the call.

- Think before you use the speaker-phone. If it is only a two-way conversation, use a headset if you need to be *hands free*.
- Don't talk louder when you are on the phone; be aware that you may do this unconsciously.
- Don't stand up or hang over the cubicle wall to have a conversation. If you and a co-worker have an agreement it's ok to have conversations "over the wall," that's fine. Just make sure to keep your voices down. Other employees do not want or need to be part of your conversation.
- Never shout a request or response to a nearby cubicle. Walk over or pick up the phone.
- Never make inappropriate or offensive sounds: burping, slurping, exaggerated yawning or tapping a pen.

Biz Tip: If you have a loud voice, get in the habit of speaking more softly. Be respectful of "noise."

Chapter in Review

The three Cs of professional cubicle behavior are:

Courtesy is awareness of the world around you and the impact that your behavior has on the others with whom you share space while at work.

Clutter in your workspace shows anyone who walks by your level of professionalism. Less is more.

Chat time is about noise control for the comfort and productivity of those around you.

WATCH, ASSESS, REACT

This chapter, while short, has three of the most important tips to help you in your transition. It can be overwhelming when we make a change in our career. These changes usually entail new job responsibilities, new co-workers to get to know, new supervisors and new outside suppliers. And if you're moving into management and having staff report to you, it becomes even more of a challenge.

Know and understand you will make some mistakes. That's fine as long as you can admit you made a mistake and learn from it. Every new position or added responsibility opens the door for learning, growing and building your career success.

Power of Observation
Observation is the act of noticing, perceiving, watching, and paying attention to see or learn something.

This is the one step I have seen so many people skip! They take on the new job and start to make changes or make suggestions to change things before they even understand the "why" behind the ways things are currently structured or done. This approach is one of the fastest ways to introduce conflict into a department. Take the time to learn and understand how things are done before you attempt to change things.

Here are a few simple tips that can aid you in developing this highly valuable skill:

- Ask questions, lots of them. Find out the "why."
- Talk to the people who are doing the actual work. Understand why policies and procedures are in place.
- Ask what would make their job easier or more efficient, what would they recommend and why.
- Try doing the task yourself to better understand the process.
- Keep an open mind – things may not need to be changed, just tweaked a bit.
- If you do have a better way or an idea, share it with others and see if it is well received and viable. Also, be open to

change your original thoughts based on feedback you receive.

> **Biz Tip:** Don't change things unless you absolutely understand how your suggested change will impact the employees and the department's policies and procedures.

As the "new kid on the block" come in softly and confidently. **Watch** what is currently being done, **Assess** the current process – what works, what doesn't, then **React** to the information you have learned. Allow your powers to observe serve you so when you do move forward to make or suggest a change, you have all the information you need and can show why the change is a good business decision for both the department and the company.

Culture Clash
(unspoken words and rules)

Part of observation is listening to spoken and unspoken words. In the Communication chapter, we'll concentrate on the spoken word. For now, I'd like to focus on the tone of voice of the messages and the body language signals that are being sent between people.

A lot can be learned about the culture and the environment in which you work just by tuning in. Unspoken words are usually between individuals who know each other well or have worked together for a long time. They can be communicated in someone's behavior or reaction to situations, their tone of voice and body language. This type of communication can be positive or negative; it can be generational, peer or hierarchy based. Learn the language of the unspoken word.

As with words, unspoken rules are important to learn and understand. Rules are the customary or normal conduct or practices within the department or company. Through your power of observation, you should be able to tell what is the accepted policy or practice. Unspoken rule examples can be as simple as cubical décor, lunch, or afternoon breaks. Following the rules is crucial to your co-workers' acceptance and perception of you as a team player.

Know the rules, follow the rules, and don't make up your own rules!

> **Biz Tip:** Think sports. Rules add structure, equalize the playing field, and help to build cohesive teams. The unspoken, unwritten rules are as important as the written policy rules.

Mining a Mentor
(find, approach, value)

Mentors are the unsung heroes in our career advancement and success. They come into our lives in many ways and types. My best mentors were my direct supervisors or other experienced managers I worked with throughout my career. They took me under their wing, showed me the ropes, answered my questions, and made time to talk to me when I was facing a difficult situation. They helped me to grow-up, take on more responsibility and were the best advocates for my career advancement. That's why you need to find and develop the relationships that will bring mentors into your circle of influence.

Important aspects about being the mentee (that would be you) – you need to be open to constructive criticism, be open-minded to change, be able to admit when you are wrong and be able to ask for help when you need it.

Asking for help is not a sign of weakness, it's a sign of strength!

Information on mentors and mentees can be found in books, blogs, articles, websites, even twitter. I pulled the information below from some of these resources that will help explain the mentor – mentee relationship.

> **Biz Tip:** There is a difference between a Mentor, a Coach and a Consultant. When starting out in your career, look for some great Mentors.

In the book *The Connectors* by Maribeth Kuzmeski there is a chapter titled: Find a Mentor – The Influence that Leads, Motivates and Holds You Accountable. The chapter begins with a quote from Tom Pace that I believe defines the "why" of the importance of finding a mentor, especially in the early stages of your career.

"You need mentors in your life to take you to the places you want to go!!! Why do you need mentors? Well, it's simple. Mentors cause you to change, or stretch yourself to new limits not known before. They also give you a larger vision for your life than you can see for yourself."

The relationship between the mentor and mentee is usually one of an older, more experienced person advising and helping a less experienced and often younger person in their career growth.

When you decide to start a mentor-mentee relationship, think of it in two steps: what do you as the mentee want to gain and accomplish and what do you want in a mentor.

Mentee Check List

- Why do you want a mentor?
- What are your goals (new skills, understanding of business, etc.)? List them in order of priority.
- How can a mentor help you achieve your goals?
- How much time are you willing to commit to working with a mentor? Once a week, monthly, quarterly?
- Will you communicate face-to-face, by phone, by email, or a combination?
- Can you be flexible since connecting will be based on your mentor's schedule?
- Are you prepared to keep commitments you make with a mentor?
- How will you track your goal achievements?

- Will you maintain your focus and enthusiasm towards this process and relationship building?
- Are you open to feedback and suggestions for improvement?

Mentor Qualities Checklist

- Does this person have the skills and experience you are looking for?
- Will this person have time in their schedule to work with you?
- Is this someone you will be comfortable talking to and sharing your ideas and areas of growth?
- Do you like this person?
- Do you believe this person is a good listener and has the desire to take on a mentee?
- Do you have trust in this person?
- Will this person be able to consistently challenge you?
- Will this person encourage you and provide the guidance you need to achieve your goals?
- Is this person respected within the organization?

How to Find a Mentor

Organizations – Through a professional or trade organization, you may find someone who meets your qualifications and is willing to become your mentor. If you do not belong to such a group, you might consider joining one for several reasons: to find a mentor, to network, to take advantage of educational sessions. Professional organizations are important if your field or position requires continuing education units to maintain your degree or certification.

Referrals – Is there someone at work whom you admire, respect, and has made an impact with their insight and perceptiveness? It could be someone higher up in your department or division, perhaps someone from a different area or the company, or it could be an individual who isn't currently an executive but has lots of experience. Is there someone from outside your company that a friend or family member could recommend?

Here are some additional articles you might find helpful on mentoring:

Inc. Magazine on-line: How to Find a Business Mentor.
http://www.inc.com/guides/how-to-find-a-business-mentor.html

Other websites:
http://www.topsuccesssite.com

Books by Lois Zachary with Lory A. Fischler include *The Mentee's Guide, The Mentor's Guide,* and *Creating a Mentoring Culture.*

Chapter in Review

Three important transition tips:

Power of Observation – Allow your powers to observe serve you so when you move forward to make or suggest a change, you have all the information you need and can show why the change is a good business decision for both the department and the company.

Observe your work community – the people and the physical environment. Learn the spoken and unspoken rules. Make your transition softly, confidently, and successfully. You'll have the power to do so.

Mentoring is a professional relationship in which an experienced person (mentor) helps the mentee in developing skills and knowledge that will improve the mentee's professional and personal growth. Find a mentor or just be open to the idea that many of the experienced managers you work with can be that "unsung hero" to you.

R.E.S.P.E.C.T.

When I talk to people about what "respect" means in the workplace, I get a wide range of comments, definitions, and head shaking. So, it's clear that a chapter on the subject is valuable for a new associate. The challenge is how to make a truly complex subject simple.

You may have heard the song "Respect," the 1967 hit and signature song for R&B singer Aretha Franklin. It was my inspiration for this acronym that helps define respect. Each word begins with a definition taken from Random House Webster's College Dictionary, 1991. You may think of other words that work for you and that's great. What does respect mean to you?

Receptive – "having the quality of receiving, taking in or admitting, 2) able or quick to receive knowledge, ideas, etc., 3) willing or inclined to receive suggestions, offers, etc."

When you are receptive you pay attention to the world around you, listen to and engage with co-workers, and keep an open mind. Sometimes we think we are right and let our ego get in the way. As a human resource manager once said, "lose the attitude" and become a receptive person.

<u>Ethics</u> – "a system or set of moral principles, 2) the rules of conduct recognized in respect to a particular class of human actions or governing a particular group, culture, etc.: *medical ethics,* 3) the branch of philosophy dealing with values relating to human conduct with respect to rightness and wrongness of actions and the goodness and badness of motives and ends, 4) moral principles as of an individual: *His ethics forbade betrayal of a confidence.*"

What exactly is a set of moral principles? Most companies have an ethics statement about how they conduct business. The example I use with my students, as it relates to the Hospitality Industry, has to do with a FAM Trip (familiarization trip or a hosted buyer event).

A hotel or a city invites meeting managers to visit and become familiar with their site or city hoping these individuals will bring business. These excursions are usually paid for by the hotel or city. A question of ethics arises if you accept an invitation, knowing that your company will not plan an event in that location. You only go because you want a free weekend away. Doing so is considered unethical in the Hospitality Industry. A FAM Trip is not a mini-vacation; it is a business trip.

I've had students ask me, "What if maybe someday in the future we might go to that location, can I still go?" If you will not be planning an event at the location within the next 12 months, then you don't go. Ethics and ethical behavior are black and white and not shades of gray.

It's important that you know your company's ethics statement and rules. If a situation arises and you aren't sure what the ethical response would be, ask your supervisor or human resource manager.

<u>S</u>elf-control – "restraint of oneself or one's actions, feelings, etc."

Before getting offended or being indignant about a person's behavior or communication style, give them the benefit of the doubt. Many times, a person is not even aware they are doing "something wrong" in the eyes of others. Based on where they stand, their behavior probably makes perfect sense.

Think before you speak and react.

Polite – "showing good manners toward others, as in behavior or speech; courteous: *a polite reply,* 2) refined or cultured: *polite society,* 3) of a refined or elegant kind: *polite learning.*"

Small courtesies go a long way. Acknowledge co-workers; a simple "good morning" or "good night" lets the person know you are aware of them. We all like to be recognized! Try adding the words "please" and "thank-you" to your requests of others. Use the person's name. It makes them feel like they matter. Hold the door open for someone. Smile. I bet you could list 10 more things you could do to be more polite at work.

<u>Esteem</u> – "to regard highly or favorably; regard with respect or admiration, 2) favorable opinion or judgment; respect or regard: *to hold a person in esteem.*"

I like this term. What it brings to mind is a select group of individuals with whom I had the privilege to work. These were the people who taught me and were great role models and mentors. I held them in "high esteem."

Who do you hold in high esteem: a professor, manager, spiritual leader, relative? These are the people who helped you to grow. Look around; who are the individuals that can help you now to develop in your career? Most likely, you already respect them and hold them in esteem.

<u>C</u>onsider – "to think carefully about, esp. in order to make a decision; contemplate; ponder, 2) to regard with respect or thoughtfulness; show consideration for; to consider other people's feelings."

This is the next step after Receptive. You have listened and taken in the information, had an open dialogue, asked questions, and have a good understanding. You are now in the consider stage. It's time to think carefully before you respond. You always want to respond thoughtfully and to consider the feeling of others.

<u>T</u>hanks – "to express gratitude or appreciation to, 2) a grateful feeling or acknowledgment of a kindness, favor or the like, expressed by words or otherwise."

This is an important word that expresses so much feeling. Sometimes I think it's a lost art! It's so easy to say, "thank you" to others who have helped you in some way.

Say "thank you" to someone when they: hold a door for you, get you the information you asked for, bring you lunch or a coffee, support you in a meeting, or return your phone call. The list could go on and on. What are some other reasons to extend a thank you?

A simple thank you can be a verbal response, an email, phone call, or a handwritten note.

Make it a practice to say thank you as part of your daily routine; it goes a long way and people appreciate it more than you will ever know.

> **Biz Tip:** These behaviors govern how we act, communicate and interact with others every day. It's how good business is done.

Four Generations in the Workplace
Why R.E.S.P.E.C.T. Makes It Work

Men resemble their times more so than their fathers.

> Ibn Khaldun, 1332-1406, Arab Philosopher and Demographer

R.E.S.P.E.C.T. - what does it have to do with business today? A lot. One of the most frequent complaints I hear when consulting with businesses is that there is not enough civility and respect in the workplace. But work is exactly where we need to practice it.

The problem is, each of us has a different idea of what R.E.S.P.E.C.T. looks like. We have our own ideas of acceptable behavior based on our age, up-bringing, education, and other factors that shaped us. With up to four generations in the workplace today, it's easy to see how misunderstandings and conflict occur.

One of the biggest challenges facing today's management is blending the four generations into cohesive working teams. As a new campus recruit or newly promoted employee, it's important to recognize that differences exist among the generations. It's those differences that can help explain the behaviors and perceptions you might see from others. That's why this subject is under the R.E.S.P.E.C.T. chapter. Respect each generation and find common ground to learn from one another.

There are many books and resources on generational differences. I encourage you to read up and get a better understanding of each generation so that you can be effective in the workplace. In this chapter, I hope to plant the *seeds of curiosity* and provide a high level look at what shapes us. Keep in mind these are generalities, not hard and fast rules that apply to every person in each generation.

Things to consider in a blended generational work environment:

- Start by being aware that differences exist and don't jump to conclusions about another's behavior.
- Dates for each generation are not set in stone; depending on the source, the years can vary slightly.
- Each generation has shared historical and social experiences like current. events, social and economic trends, pop culture, (music/fashion/movies) etc.
- These shared historical and social experiences shape values both at work and in private life.
- Accept how all of the above impacts expectations and behaviors in the workplace.

- Language. Each generation has its own lexicon and slang. It's easy to leave someone out of the conversation when we use it. What should you do? Ask the person to explain what they meant before you make a judgment. This allows for sharing experiences and opens both of you to understanding one another.

Multi-Generational Challenges:

- Communication preferences; ask how a person would like to receive communication – not everyone likes a text message.
- Definition of work "day" – the Millennials and Gen Xers prefer flexible hours and days although the motivation is different. Millennials relate work to a "lifestyle" they are living. Gen Xer's lifestyle has also moved from the structured 8-5 work day, but their movement is due to caring for aging parents.
- Work assignments – some respond better to a planned way of doing things, others like the freedom to approach the tasks in a manner they feel suits their working style.

- Promotional opportunities – making sure everyone understands the skills and qualifications required to be considered for promotion. Seniority level or length of employment doesn't always mean you get promoted.
- Office policies – how to execute and implement policies and procedures, especially if one is not in agreement with the change. Some individuals will adapt, while others will challenge the process.

Employees of all generations view work as an extension of themselves:

- Seek personal fulfillment and satisfaction from their job.
- Want compensation that is fair in the current marketplace.
- Highest indicator of job satisfaction among all generations is feeling valued for the work they perform.
- The workplace culture cultivated by the organization and its managers directly relates to the overall job satisfaction felt by all employees. A majority (over 70%) of employees prefer a work environment where they feel supported, recognized, and appreciated.

- Career development is a high priority among all generations; only half of them feel their current employer does a good job of supporting this interest.
- Offering a flexible work schedule to accommodate individuals goes a long way with employees in each generation.
- Seven out of 10 workers would like to set their own work hours, as long as the work that needs to get done is done at the highest quality and on time.

Biz Tip: Keep in mind that we all can make changes in our behavior to get along better with others. But change isn't always easy.

Chapter in Review

As you go about changing your awareness and your behavior to create a more productive and harmonious work environment, remember it takes time.

For example: to start a new behavior – you must practice that behavior for 21 days to begin a new pattern.

It takes 100 days for the pattern to become automatic – continue to practice the new behavior to really make it stick.

Understand the different generations in your workplace. Use R.E.S.P.E.C.T. to develop better working relationships and to promote a more profitable business environment.

Biz Tip: Always be considerate. Always be respectful. Always be polite.

COMMUNICATIONS

"The newest computer can merely compound, at speed, the oldest problem in the relations between human beings, and in the end the communicator will be confronted with the old problem, of what to say and how to say it."   Edward R. Murrow, American news broadcaster

The need to effectively communicate in the workplace has not changed in the 21st century. What has changed is the cultural and technological diversity:

Age – currently there are four generations in the workforce, each with their own preferences and comfort in communication styles.

Nationalities – we are a multi-cultural nation and that brings a wide range of customs, languages, and work ethics to the workplace.

- Technologies – from email to twitter the challenge is how best to use these tools.

- Working environments – is it a building you go to, a home office, or a virtual office?
- International companies – customs, time zones, written word, language differences and difficulty in building relationships.

As we talk about communication, I'd like you to visualize a bicycle wheel and you are the center of it. Every spoke that fans out from you represents individuals in other departments, mangers, team members, company divisions, customers, and outside vendors. You may need to communicate with these people to complete your job responsibilities. You might engage with them daily, weekly, monthly, or only yearly, but they are all vital to how your company does business day-to-day and how you succeed at your job.

Your challenge is to understand who you need to communicate with and why. Then, keeping the above diversities in mind, determine how best to communicate.

Communication is hard work, and it is a behavioral skill well worth learning.

This chapter's tips are on two aspects of communication:

- Verbal - speaking and listening: face-to-face, phone, or voice mail.
- Written - words you write: paper, email, Twitter, Facebook, etc.

Verbal Communication

Google "verbal communication" and you will get over 9,670,000 hits! In the simplest of terms, verbal communication is your voice that makes sounds that are converted to words that convey a message to another person. This can be face-to-face, by phone, through voice mail, on Face Time, Skype, live video, or conference call, etc. Basically, anytime you are speaking and someone can hear your voice you are sending a "verbal message."

Verbal messages can bring a range of challenges and communication breakdowns. Some of these are: bad choice of words, misunderstood message, different point of view, language difficulty, and poor communication skills. Even your social class, education level, or where you live can create misunderstanding when the other person doesn't interpret your message as you intended.

The delivery system (that's you) is what creates communication breakdowns. However, you can get your message across regardless of the circumstances. Even if you are angry, upset, confused or what have you, effective communication is within your ability. Real communication starts with these two important principles:

1st A person's perception is their reality. How a person looks at a situation is how they are going to respond in that moment – that's what is real to them. You don't have to like it or agree with their response, but you do have to accept it because that's what is true for that person.

2nd The situation (person, place, or thing) *does not* dictate your response. You and only you have the choice of how you will respond. And your reaction, i.e. tone of voice, words and phrases used and even your non-verbal body language, has an impact on the outcome of the situation at hand.

Biz Tip: Don't get confused between the words agree and accept. *Agree* is to be of one mind; harmonize in opinion or feeling. *Accept* is to accommodate or reconcile oneself to: accept the situation. (Random House Webster College Dictionary)

Verbal communications has to do with politeness, respect, self-control, good manners, and an open mind!

"Words are the most powerful drug used by mankind."   Rudyard Kipling, English Writer

Key points on an effective verbal delivery system:

- Don't discount the power of your words. Think before you speak. Once the words are out, you can't get them back.
- Keep the volume of your voice moderate at all times; a loud voice can be annoying, intimidating or threatening.
- Make sure you need to speak; sometimes silence can be kinder and more considerate than words.
- Avoid going off on a tangent.
- Stop when you have made your point and let the other person speak.
- Never yell at anybody.
- You can be angry and still be civil; it's the words used and tone of voice.
- Never utter unkind words regarding a person's racial, national, sexual, or gender identity.
- Never use profanities; fastest way to offend someone.

- Never embarrass.

Don't say mean words or gossip about others. It can hurt their reputation and their feelings if the words get back to them. Even worse, this can make you look untrustworthy, i.e. if you are willing to bad-mouth others then you're likely to bad-mouth me as well.

Good way to end this section on verbal and listening communication is summed up in these two great quotes:

Two monologues do not make a dialogue.
Jeffrey L. Daly - American architect

The ability to speak eloquently is not to be confused with having something to say.
Michael P. Hart, from Areia Gloris/Yes to Riches/Top 7 Communication Quotes

Learning to Listen
"If you just communicate, you can get by. But if you skillfully communicate, you can work miracles."
Jim Rohn, American business philosopher and author

What is listening? Listening is the skill that correctly receives and understands verbal messages during the communication process. We use our ears to *hear sounds* that we translate into words. We use our mind to interpret the words to the message to what we think is being sent.

Why is listening important? Verbal messages can easily be misinterpreted. When this happens, the sender of the message can become frustrated, irritated, or even angry.

Even more importantly, the speaker could walk away thinking you don't have the capability to understand what's been said or you simply don't care. Leaving this type of impression is not good for your reputation, particularly if the speaker is your boss, a senior executive, or a major client. The end result is bad decisions may be made on information that was interpreted incorrectly. Excellent listening skills can prevent this type of a mishap at work.

Remember, communication is never one-way. As a listener, you are even more responsible than the speaker for ensuring communication occurs. Why? Well, the speaker can only communicate when you allow his or her words to get through. Otherwise, the speaker is merely making sounds . . . blah, blah, blah; there is no communication. True communication is about interaction and striving to understand.

How to be a better listener? The easiest approach is to always be receptive to the other person. In *Choosing Civility, The Twenty-five Rules of Considerate Conduct,* P. M. Forni defines it as:

"Receptivity is the willingness to listen to the other person and consider what he's saying. It's the willingness to take in (receive) what the other person knows, believes, thinks, and feels. It's the willingness to pay attention, to concentrate, to weigh, to evaluate, to mull over.

The receptive person is willing to give the other person a chance to get through; he's willing to cooperate in the communication process. This doesn't mean he agrees with what he hears; it only means he will consider it."

Practice these few tips until they become part of your everyday behavior and style.

- Plan to listen – listen with no other purpose than to listen. Keep an open mind. Listen carefully. Sometimes this is not easy if we have already made up our mind on what we believe the outcome should be. Listening with an open mind allows you to ask better questions, get information that you may not have been aware of, and move you toward better decision making. You may gain valuable information and often a better understanding of where the other person is coming from.

- Indicate you are listening, say something like, "I wasn't aware of that" or "That's interesting, tell me more."
- Answer questions raised by the other person. Don't be afraid to answer and share information (unless it's confidential to the company). If you don't have the answer, let them know you will get it, get back to them in a reasonable time, and then keep your commitment.
- Ask questions to clarify what the other person means if you are unsure. Be clear on where you are confused or unsure of their meaning. Don't be vague!
- Use the open-ended question technique – don't ask a question that can be responded to with either a yes or no.
- No need to rush to agree or disagree. It's better to show you understand the issues at hand. This helps the person

to know you have listened. An easy way to get clarification is to use the technique of restating what you believe the other person has said. An example might be "Mary, let me see if I understood what you meant regarding final deadlines. The project needs to be 100% complete by the last Friday of this month."

> **Biz Tip:** *"Much of the conflict in our lives can be explained by one simple but unhappy fact: we don't really listen to each other."* Michael P. Nichols, author of *The Lost Art of Listening*

The Business Call

Today we almost always expect to get the person's voice mail and not the actual person when we call. If we do get a live person, it can throw us off. In either case, take the time to prepare for your call. It will save you time and promote good relationships.

Placing the call:
- Prepare by writing down any specific questions and topics to cover. This will help keep the conversation on track and on time.

- Have available facts, figures and documentation needed; saves time and you look organized and prepared.
- Blank paper or notebook and pen for taking notes.
- When using a computer to take notes, let the other person know you will be typing so the sound of the keys will not be distracting or give the impression you are working on something other than the conversation.
- Calendar to set follow-up dates – not to overbook.
- Always identify yourself: first and last name and company to reinforce name recognition.
- Quickly explain reason for call.
- When it's an unscheduled call, always ask if it's a good time to talk. If not, ask when would be a better time to call back.
- After the call, send a summary email. Highlight key points/decisions made, follow-up actions/who is responsible and date and time of next meeting or call.

Wrong numbers:
- Don't hang up, say, "I'm sorry. I must have dialed the wrong number."

- Give the number you called so you don't make the same mistake twice.

Put on Hold:
- If you are pressed for time, tell the gatekeeper you would like to leave a message or be transferred to the person's voice mail.
- If on hold more than 3 minutes, it is ok to hang up and call back later.
- Be courteous when you connect with the person. Politely say you could not hold; no explanation is required.

Speaker Phone/Conference Call:
- Immediately tell the person(s) on the other end that you are using a speakerphone and ask if it is "ok."
- Have each person introduce themselves so all on the call can identify names and voices.
- When someone joins the conversation after the initial introductions, be sure to politely stop the conversation and introduce the new person. It's good manners to be sure everyone knows who is on the call at all times.
- Use a person's name during the call – "James, Nancy has a question for

you." or "This is Sandy and I would like to comment on. . . "

- Close the office door during the call. If you don't have an office, see if a meeting room is available that does have a door.
- When on a conference call, remember your background noise can be disruptive to others, so mute your phone when you are not speaking.

Phone-Call Faux Pas – Common mistakes to avoid:

- Don't do other things at your desk while talking, like typing or shuffling papers. Concentrate on the conversation and listen; when you are doing other things you are not listening.
- No eating while on the phone.
- Turn off music.
- Never chew gum while talking on the phone.
- Don't sneeze, blow your nose, or cough into the receiver. Either excuse yourself for a moment or turn your head away.
- Gently put the receiver down on the desk if you have to during the conversation.

- Be careful not to address a business associate by their first name in sentence after sentence; it sounds insincere and patronizing.
- Don't answer a phone call when in a meeting or place a person on "hold" to take another call during a conversation.
- Never place someone on "hold" without permission.
- Don't stalk a co-worker while they are on the phone; come back later.

Answering Business Calls:
- Always try to answer the phone. Incoming calls answered by a person instead of a machine make a good impression for both you and the company.
- Forget personal problems. Your voice should sound pleasant and calm when you answer the phone. Remember, you are speaking for the company, not yourself.
- Answer the phone promptly – by the third ring if possible.
- Answer with something like "This is Susan White speaking. How may I help you?"

- If you are really busy, or in the middle of a project, don't take the call, or if you do, let the person know you can't talk now and set up a time that works for both of you.

Returning Calls:
- Return calls as soon as possible. Twenty-four hours is as long as a call can go unreturned without violating the precepts of good manners.

Leaving a Voice Mail Message:
Treat recording devises with good manners. A message left in an upbeat tone of voice gives the recipient of the call confidence in both you and your company; an irritated tone does quite the opposite.

- Don't speak too fast – slow down, especially when you leave the return phone number.
- Always leave your name, the company name, and the return phone number twice during the message. Once at the beginning and again at the end.
- Give enough information in the message – provide the reason for the call, keep it short and to the point. No rambling messages!

- Assume the person will answer – be prepared to have a conversation.
- Don't fill up another person's voice mailbox. One message per day is sufficient.
- Never use a voice system to avoid a difficult conversation.

Your Recorded Voice Mail Greeting:
- Keep the tone of your voice upbeat.
- Speak naturally and with an even pace; not too fast or too slow.
- Keep your message simple and short. "Hi, this is Sally Smith. Sorry I'm unable to take your call at this time. Please leave a brief message and a return phone number and I will get back to you as soon as I am able."
- You may want to update your message daily if you are out of the office and give a date when the call will be returned.
- When on vacation or extended time out of the office, leave the name and phone number of someone they can contact during your absence. Also, leave your return date to the office or when they can expect a return call from you.

Cell Phone:

- Put it away and on silent mode when in meetings or face-to-face conversations.

- It is rude and <u>not ok</u> to read/respond to an email, text, or to IM someone while you are face-to-face with another person or in a meeting.

- If you must look at or answer your phone, excuse yourself for a minute so you don't send the message that the person(s) you are with is not as important as the email, text or call.

- When away from your desk, don't use the phone if it will bother people around you. Move to a place that is private.

- Absolutely never say anything confidential, personal, or private if others can overhear you. Instead arrange to call the person back at a later time.

- Speak quietly – people don't want to hear your conversation; it's distracting.

- Don't overdo it. A brief conversation isn't likely to disturb anyone, but an hour of continuous use may drive those around you crazy.

- Be safe when using the cell phone. That means while driving or walking.

Don't stop suddenly to write, text or answer the phone. Your inattention or lack of awareness to your surroundings and environment could impact another person.

Biz Tip: Know your company's policy regarding the use of cell phones especially if used in a vehicle while on company business.

Good Writing

You don't write because you want to say something; you write because you've got something to say.   F. Scott Fitzgerald, American author

This quote from Barbara Pachter, business communications consultant and etiquette expert, says it all. *"Words have power, and written words have lasting power."* The way we communicate has changed dramatically in the last decade thanks to email, voice mail and social networking sites. In the business world, one thing has not changed; the importance of our words and the need to write them clearly and effectively.

When you put your thoughts in writing, it's a concrete representation of your command of the language, your writing skills and your professionalism. Your writing says a lot about you and the company you represent.

Good writing must meet the four C's. Ask yourself, is it:
- **Correct?** Does it accurately describe the situation?
- **Clear?** Have you said what you intended to say?
- **Coherent?** Will the reader understand?
- **Clean?** Are there any misspelled words or grammatical mistakes?

Key points to successful letter writing are keeping it straightforward and uncomplicated.
- Organize your thoughts before you start. Always write a rough draft.
- Write a good opening sentence. If you don't capture their attention, they may not read the rest.
- Use the proper title of the person with whom you are corresponding. It can be insulting to the person if their title is incorrect.
- Address them by their full name, unless your relationship warrants more familiarity.

- Verify their name is spelled correctly. Few things are more annoying than seeing your name misspelled.
- Write in the first person unless the letter is representing the company as a whole.
- Be natural; write in complete sentences, leave out interjections and excessive use of pronouns.
- Keep it short; write only what is needed to get the message across. Include important information. Eliminate extra words.
- Use bullet points when possible.
- Avoid clichés and buzzwords; use everyday language.
- Avoid technical jargon and specialized language unless you are certain the reader is familiar with the field.
- Proofread. Read and read again for spelling, grammar and punctuation errors. Never rely totally on the computer's spelling and grammar checks. "Pleas sea hour lay test add" will pass as will "Please see our latest ad."
- Read it out loud to someone or yourself. Reading out loud will help to catch awkward, cumbersome phrasing and omitted words.

- Use humor thoughtfully and selectively. What is funny to one can be offensive to another.
- Avoid negative phasing – "You forgot to attached the waiver." vs. "Please remember to include the waiver in the future."
- Make sure you communicate correctly for the intended reader. A letter to a colleague would be written differently than one to a senior executive.

> **Biz Tip:** Words are things. Each word conveys a specific meaning. The difference in words can be subtle – choose them wisely.

Emails, Text, and IM Messages:
RU, LOL, TTYL. It looks like a foreign language or a secret code, but it's a new form of writing. Today our need for speed – fast internet, fast downloads, fast phone connections – has given way to a fast way to write, text, or IM a person. This may be acceptable on a social level, but it is not acceptable in the business world. The person receiving the message needs to comprehend what you are saying and not everyone understands this new form of writing.

The rules of good writing apply to email, text and IM messages as well. Whether you are using a cell phone, tablet, laptop, or desktop, remember to start with the basics and don't use the new word shortcuts.

- Understand the rules of writing still apply.
- Follow company guidelines on the appropriate use of email.
- Don't contribute to email overload. Respect others' "electronic space."
- Appropriate use of Cc's and Bcc's – who really needs to see the message?
- Not all Cc's on an email need to see the reply. For example, if it's just a "Thanks" only the person who sent the email should be on the reply. The biggest complaint with email is un-necessary emails due to "reply all." Think who really needs to read and know the information in the email.
- Don't give out someone's email address without permission.
- Don't assume that everybody wants to correspond by email, text or IM. Always ask the person what is their preferred way to communicate.
- Check your email regularly.

- Respond in a reasonable amount of time; best practice is within 24 hours.
- Do not mark urgent, unless it is.
- Never forward unless you know it would be appropriate.
- Use the "out of office" auto reply.
- Use "return receipt" only when necessary.
- Keep messages short and simple.
- Short paragraphs or bullet points.
- Always use appropriate business language; no slang, jokes, or abbreviations.
- Always use the subject line.
- DON'T USE ALL CAP LETTERS – Save them for emphasis.
- Don't use emoticon faces or special characters to express your mood – happy :), sad :(, etc. It is unprofessional.
- Don't' write anything about anyone that you would not say directly to that person.
- Proofread, proofread, and proofread before you hit the send key.
- Don't send a message containing any business information that should be kept confidential.
- Don't email when upset or angry; put it in the "drafts box" and come back

to it in a few hours or the next day. Almost certainly you'll make some changes. Remember, once you hit the send key, you won't get it back, so be sure the tone is professional and not offensive.

- Don't email for important thank-you notes.

- Salutations and closings should be used if it's a new email. Once in the "reply" process, they are not technically required, but nice.

> **Biz Tip:** There is no privacy protection for emails at your job. Stop and think about the content before you hit "send."

Chapter in Review

Verbal communication – any time you are speaking and someone can hear your voice you are sending a "verbal message." Make sure the message delivered is polite, respectful, controlled, has a pleasant tone, and positive words.

Learn to Listen – Remember it's the listener who communicates, not the speaker. Communication requires a dialogue; a back-and-forth conversation.

The Business Call – Proper phone protocols are essential to how you come across as a professional and how well you represent your company.

Good Writing – When you put your thoughts in writing, it's a concrete representation of your command of the language, your writing skills and, most importantly, your professionalism. Your writing says a lot about you and the company you represent.

MEETING MASTERY – BEHAVIORS THAT MAKE A DIFFERENCE

It's easy to think you just have to show up at a meeting to make an impression – think again.

Follow these business behaviors and watch your career grow.

1. **Arrive on time.** It sounds like common sense, but think about how many meetings you have attended where the group had to wait for someone. Or worse yet, stop the meeting in progress and have to recap for the late comer. It is rude and disrespectful to the other participants to arrive late and disrupt the meeting. It's a time-waster!

2. **Dress.** Always dress appropriately for the meeting. Proper dress attire could change from a meeting held in

the office, which could be business casual, to a 5-star restaurant that requires a suit and tie.

3. **Introductions.** if there is administrative staff, always greet them and introduce yourself if you do not know them. People do not like to be ignored; be friendly and respectful. The same is true for each participant who is attending the meeting. Greet the ones you know and be sure to introduce yourself and shake hands with those you do not know.

4. **Be prepared.** There is a reason for your participation in the meeting or you would not have been invited. Know the agenda in advance and come ready to contribute to the discussion. If you are unsure of what you are expected to contribute, call the meeting organizer or your supervisor and find out. You can't be prepared if you don't know what is expected of you. Remember, never offer information/data unless you are sure it is correct and you can provide back-up documentation. Be an enthusiastic team player; listen to others, and

share information. Your reputation is on the line.

5. **Turn off your phone.** If you are expecting an "emergency" call, place your phone in silence mode and notify the meeting facilitator. If you get a call, leave the room to answer. Make sure to quietly close the door behind you. Understand when you look at your phone or emails during a meeting you are sending a very clear message that other things are more important than the meeting and its participants. Others notice you're not paying attention. *That is not okay.*

6. **Note Taking.** If you use your laptop, tablet, or phone to take notes during the meeting, let the facilitator and others know. This way, they won't think you're doing something else, like responding to emails or posting to Facebook.

7. **Pay attention.** Each person who speaks deserves your attention. This means no playing with your pen, no doodling, no staring out the window, and yes, you guessed it, no messing

with your phone (see point 5). These bad habits give the impression you are not paying attention even if you are.

8. **Side-bar conversations.** Keep to a minimum or not at all. It's distracting and rude. Covering your mouth while taking to the person next to you does not stop others from seeing and maybe hearing your conversation. You may miss something and have to ask to have it repeated. This is a waste of other people's time.

9. **Other time wasters.** If a topic or point has already been discussed, don't bring it up again unless you have something important to add. And don't add a new topic of discussion to the agenda unless approved by the meeting organizer.

10. **Clean up.** Before you leave the meeting, pick up your trash and toss it out. It's not ok to let others clean up your mess.

11. **Meetings in a restaurant.** See chapter on Avoiding Dining Disasters.

> **Biz Tip:** Maintain a professional image during the meeting: have good posture, no slouching, no grooming yourself – biting your nails, putting on lipstick, combing your hair, etc. It is inappropriate behavior; people will notice and remember.

Professional Presentations:

Most people don't like to stand up in front of an audience to give a talk or presentation. Some are even uncomfortable presenting their information in business meetings, especially in front of senior executives. Stage fright is the number one obstacle in giving a presentation. People feel nervous, get "butterflies" in their stomach, and feel like they can't remember what to say. But take heart, if you have stage fright, you are in the majority.

The most important thing you can do is to simply acknowledge that giving a presentation is an uncomfortable task for you. Notice I didn't say a weakness; it's simply an area where you need some help in developing the skills that give you the confidence to talk before a group. The uneasiness you feel just before you talk is just adrenaline, a natural "energy boost!" Any top athlete or performer has this same adrenaline energy rush that helps them to perform their best. The butter-flies you feel in the pit of your stomach are "a good thing."

The first step in improving your presentation skills is to stop thinking of it as a negative task or experience. Think of it as your chance to stand out from your colleagues and get noticed. Obviously, someone has confidence in your ability. You should be proud to have been asked to present.

These points are skills and behaviors you can learn. Master these soft skills and you will gain the confidence and polish required to give a professional presentation.

- **Organize the presentation**
  There are three clear-cut parts to any presentation: the introduction, the main body, and the conclusion. Be sure to have all three or your presen-tation will not be cohesive.

- **Introduction should tell the purpose**
  It's important during the introduc-tion to let the audience know the rea-son for the talk and what they will learn. Also, make sure you grab their

attention in the beginning. Start with a related story, quote an expert or statistic, or ask a question, such as "Did you know that Twitter already has 86% of the internet Social Media market?"

- **Main body**
  There should only be three to five main points. That's about as much as the audience can absorb and process. Backup each of the points with stories, pictures, facts, or details.

- **Conclusion**
  Make sure you have an effective close. Briefly recap the main points and end on a positive note or call to action. Following the conclusion, take questions if appropriate. Always repeat the question before giving your answer.

- **Practice**
  "Practice makes perfect," so take the time to practice the presentation out loud and in front of a mirror. The more times you practice, the more comfortable and confident you will be with the delivery of the material.

- **Physical Considerations**

  Dress appropriately for the audience you are addressing. Posture is key. Stand with your legs 4-6 inches apart to help with weight distribution and be sure to keep your shoulders back. Watch your hand gestures. Vary the volume, rate, and pitch of your voice. Make eye contact with the audience. Never point a finger at the audience; use an open hand, palm up instead.

- **Other Things**

  Be careful with humor. Arrive early to check room set-up and audiovisual equipment. Keep PowerPoint slides simple. Use a title and three bullet points per slide and go easy with the graphics.

Biz Tip: Arrive early to make sure the room is set up correctly, that your computer equipment is working and you have done a sound check if using a microphone.

Meeting Mastery - Virtual

Think showing up is enough? Think again.

- The way you show up matters
- The impressions you make can shape your career
- Follow these meeting-ready behaviors every time

Maintaining proper etiquette during virtual meetings on platforms like Zoom and Microsoft Teams is essential for productive and respectful interactions. Here are key guidelines to follow:

Before the Meeting:

- **Test Your Equipment:** Ensure your microphone, camera, and internet connection are functioning correctly to prevent technical issues during the meeting.

- **Choose an Appropriate Environment:** Select a quiet, well-lit space with a neutral background to minimize distractions.

- **Dress Appropriately:** Wear attire suitable for the meeting's context, reflecting professionalism.

- **Come Prepared:** Know the agenda, your role, and clarify expectations ahead of time. Contribute with confidence and accuracy.

During the Meeting:

- **Be Punctual:** Join the meeting on time to respect others' schedules.

- **Mute When Not Speaking:** Keep your microphone muted when not speaking to eliminate background noise.

- **Enable Video:** Turning on your camera fosters engagement and mirrors in-person interactions.

- **Maintain Professional Body Language:** Sit upright, make eye contact by looking into the camera.

- **Give Your Full Attention:** No fidgeting, doodling, or phone-checking. Your focus shows respect and professionalism.

- **Use Virtual Backgrounds Wisely:** If using a virtual background, ensure it's not distracting and aligns with the meeting's tone.

- **Participate Actively:** Engage in discussions, use the 'raise hand' feature to speak, and provide feedback through reactions when appropriate.

- **Use the Chat Box:** To ask questions, answer questions, provide feedback.

After the Meeting:

- **Provide Feedback:** If requested, offer constructive feedback to help improve future virtual meetings.

Biz Tip: Adhering to these guidelines, you contribute to a respectful and efficient virtual meeting.

Chapter in Review

Meetings are an important part of everyday business. How you show up and your participation are key to career success. The ten points in this chapter may seem like common sense, but when people don't follow them, they become the top frustrations and pet peeves for attendees. Avoid these common mistakes and faux pas.

Meeting manners count so learn them, practice them, and become a true meeting professional.

Professional presentations can be a truly scary event for many people. Chances are you will be asked, at some point in your career, to give a presentation. Now is a great time to begin working on giving one. The seven tips provided will help you to get started. If you need practice, *Toastmasters International* meetings are a learn-by-doing workshop in which participants hone their speaking and leadership skills in a no pressure atmosphere. Contact them at: http://www.toastmasters.org/

Giving an effective and polished business presentation will take you a long way in your career. Show others your professional business image, knowledge, talent, and self-confidence.

RELATIONSHIP BUILDING

The key to success in business and in life is having trustworthy, lasting and reliable relationships. Building this type of connection takes time, effort, and patience.

Technology, on the one hand, has made our lives easier; on the other, it has made the "patience" part of developing a relationship more difficult. I wish it were possible to wave a magic wand and "voila" you have a solid, long-lasting relationship – it just doesn't work that way, especially in business. Even with all the social media sites, cell phones, email, etc. it's still the face-to-face and slow building of trust that turns these connections into a solid relationship.

This chapter's tips are about workplace behaviors that can aid you in building solid business relationships:

1. 13 Professional behaviors that make a difference.

2. Working Assertive, Not Aggressive

3. Chapter Review – Class Act! Are you considered a class act at work?

Professional Workplace Behavior

Have you ever observed a co-worker behaving inappropriately in a meeting? Have you seen a co-worker mistreat or disregard another co-worker? If so, then you know how important professional behavior is in the workplace.

It's not just about proper manners or correct protocols. It's about how we act and treat each other at work. Based on research conducted by Harvard University, The Carnegie Foundation, and The Stanford Research Institute, technical skills and knowledge account for 15% of the reason you get a job, keep a job, and advance in a job. *85% percent of your job success is connected to your people skills.*

The points below by P.M. Forni, co-founder of the Johns Hopkins Civility Project, from his book *Choosing Civility* are skills and behaviors you can learn. Master these soft skills and you will build solid and lasting business relationships that will certainly help in your career success.

- Pay Attention and Acknowledge Others. When you are with others, pay attention to the world around you. Only after you notice who and what is around you can you be concerned for others. A simple example is paying attention while on your cell phone! I'm sure you have seen the YouTube videos of people looking at their phone and walking into things, people have even fallen off train platforms. Now that's scary. To acknowledge others is so easy; it's a smile, eye contact, nod of the head, good morning, afternoon, or evening greeting.

- Listen. Pay attention to what's been said. Make sure you understand correctly. Ask questions to clarify. Funny how this communication skill keeps coming up – it's important to master it!

- Be Inclusive. One of our desires is to be accepted by others. Attitudes and words that exclude rather than include are rarely funny and often hurtful. Include those around you in conversation or ask other employees to go to lunch.

- Speak Kindheartedly. Speak with consideration and thoughtfulness. Be aware that you are speaking to a real human being. Watch the words and how you say them when speaking with others. Words and tone of voice matter!

- Don't Speak Badly of Others. This means NO GOSSIP. If you can't say something positive about the person or if you can't say it to their face, then don't say anything at all.

- Respect Others' Opinions. Respect for the opinions of co-workers isn't always easy. It requires self-esteem, self-control, tolerance, fairness, sensitivity, and generosity. You don't have to agree with their views, but you do have to accept that it's okay for them to have an opinion different from yours.

- Be Open-minded. This one is hard. Keep in mind the possibility that at any moment, you might be wrong and someone else could be right. When you realize you are wrong, you show your strength. Admit it in a gracious way and show your self-confidence.

- Respect Other People's Time. We respect other people's time when we learn to value it as much as we value our own. Punctuality is nonnegotiable.

1. Don't cancel an appointment at the last moment unless it's truly an emergency.

2. When you make a call, always ask, "Am I disturbing you" or "Do you have a few minutes to talk now?"

3. Always respect the deadlines to which you have agreed.

4. Don't cut short a scheduled meeting on a whim or because it would be more convenient for you. The other person may need all the scheduled time.

- Apologize Earnestly. Sincere apologies remain one of the most valuable tools in building relationships. Don't expect to be forgiven right away; it might take a while so have patience. Give the person some time to process the situation. Don't make apologizing a scary encounter. Keep it simple, straightforward, and heartfelt. Three steps are all it takes to apologize:

1. Tell the person you are sorry for whatever the mistake or issue is you helped to create and,

2. That you understand the negative or hurtful impact it has had on them and,

3. What you are going to do to correct it now or in the future.

- Avoid Personal Questions. Most of us have parts of our lives we want to keep private. Privacy-probing questions can unsettle, embarrass, and even upset co-workers.

- Refrain From Complaining. What's wrong with complaining? It concentrates on problems rather than solutions and reinforces a pessimistic outlook. It is bad for those around you because it spreads your pessimism to them. Let go of unproductive complaining.

- Accept and Give Constructive Criticism. To criticize is a serious business and sometimes an awesome responsibility. Before speaking, make sure your intention is to help with a problem and not to humiliate, manipulate, settle a score, or get payback.

- Don't Shift Responsibility and Blame. This means if you created the problem, then admit it and don't try to shift the blame to others. This causes the person who is not at fault to think maybe something is wrong with their request or it can cause anger or resentment when they know they are right.

> **Biz Tip:** Professional business behavior is being civil to others in all your interactions. It's integrating a code of behavior based on Respect, Restraint, and Responsibility. Remember to include these three "R's" in all your interactions with co-workers, clients and outside vendors and suppliers.

Early in my career, I was working for a large retail company in their corporate headquarters. During one of my annual reviews, it was brought to my attention that others perceived my behavior as "aggressive." WOW. That was an eye-opener. I thought I was being assertive, not aggressive. If I wanted my career to continue to grow, I knew I would need to make some changes. But how and where should I begin?

I started by observing other employees. I watched how they behaved, how they responded to problems, and how they interacted with higher-level executives. I noticed the difference in aggressive versus assertive behavior was two-fold. It involved both verbal and physical language. By observing these two aspects, it became clear to me who would be advancing in their careers and who would not, who was building relationships and who was not.

I began to change my words, tone, and delivery of my messages. I made changes in my body language and I learned to listen to what was being said. It was amazing what happened when I began to understand where the other person was coming from through my own positive behavior.

But I must admit my transformation from aggressive to assertive was gradual. It was a lot of trial and error and quite a bit of frustration. By sharing what I learned, I hope it will make the transition much easier for you.

- The spoken word. Words can have a positive or a negative impact on the person with whom you are communicating. Watch the words you speak. You can choose less offensive words and still get your point across. For example: Being aggressive, you might say "I can't believe you missed another deadline. You're putting the entire project at risk." An assertive response could be, "John, I see you missed your due date again. I know you understand the importance of completing the project on time. Is there some way the team can help you meet these dates?"

- Next is the delivery of your message. It comes from the tone of voice that you use. Is your tone positive, angry, condescending, understanding, sarcastic, kind, excited, empathic, or happy? The tone reinforces the words you use. Think of the last conversation you had that was uncomfortable for you. What words and tone did the other person use and how did you react?

You can be angry or frustrated and still use positive words and tone to get your message across. The delivery will be more impactful and more effective if it does not put the listener in a defensive mode that closes them off to what you are saying. Others will like working with you because you can get your point across and be firm in your convictions without attacking or putting them down.

> **Biz Tip:** Anger can feed anger. Best way to defuse an angry situation is to step back and listen. Focus on the problem – not the person.

- Body language is the third part of aggressive versus assertive behavior. Your words may say one thing, but people believe what your body is communicating.

  What is aggressive body language? In your facial expressions, it might be a crunched forehead, tight mouth, or squinty eyes; in your arms, are they folded, clenched fists, exaggerated movements, or pointing a finger; your posture, is it stiff, leaning forward and in their face, or turned away in indifference. Be relaxed within yourself so your body language remains natural and calm.

If you've now decided you need to work on your aggressiveness, you must practice the new behavior for 21 days for it to begin to take hold and 100 days for it to become automatic. Then your new words, tone, and body language will be natural to you.

Are the changes worth it? Take it from me, they are. Today's work environment is highly competitive both within a company as well as for those seeking employment. Learning and understanding what assertive behavior is can really help you build relationships and your career. Be assertive and be a step ahead of your competition!

Biz Tip: Show respect and consideration to all. It's a significant part of building strong business relationships and cohesive and successful teams.

Chapter Review

Class Act? Are You Considered a Class Act at Work?

"Charm is the ability to make someone else think that both of you are wonderful."
Edgar Magnin, Rabbi & Spiritual Leader

I chose this article I wrote in March 2013 for the chapter review because it takes the topics, 13 Professional Behaviors and Working Assertive, Not Aggressive and sums up what can happen when you integrate them into your daily behavior and actions. They are the stepping stones to becoming a "Class Act."

You have probably heard the term "he (or she) is a class act." If you took a moment right now, I bet you could think of a person you would call a class act. When I think about it, I think of Jacqueline Kennedy, actor Will Smith, Bill Gates, Warren Buffett, and several individuals for whom I have had the pleasure to work. So, what makes up a "class act?"

Author Jack Canfield, in his book *The Success Principles,* writes that to become a class act one must *"Strive to become the kind of person who acts with class, who becomes known as a class act, and who attracts other people with class to his or her sphere of influence."* You do that with a change in attitude, perspective, and behavior.

- One distinctive behavior a "class act" exhibits is taking responsibility for their actions.
- Being honest about the results of their decisions and actions, whether successful or not.
- Showing respect and appreciation toward others. In short, don't gossip or make mean and petty remarks.
- In difficult situations, remain calm and in control. Don't lose your temper or act out.

- Allow others to assist in the problem-solving process. This is called "grace under pressure."
- Find a "class act" in your own life. Study how he or she behaves in different situations.
- Notice they are able to make others feel included and respected for their individual contributions, especially during difficult times.
- Class Acts help others to feel good about themselves and to feel appreciated. Just by being who they are – a great role model, they inspire people to make changes in their behavior and to raise their standard of performance.
- They are the leaders who help increase the confidence, capabilities, esteem, and performance of others by living by their own high standards. People simply want to be like them.

How do you compare with the characteristics above? Why should you even consider this? Because being a "class act" will help you succeed in business and in life. It's a major part of building relationships. People like to do business with people they respect, trust, like and want to be around. That seems like reason enough for me.

> **Biz Tip:** Our ability to relate and connect to others is part of being successful and brings enjoyment to the work day.

DINING FOR DOLLAR$
AVOIDING DINING DISASTERS

This chapter was written by my dear friend, Mary Jean Billingsley, M. Ed. of Lasting Impressions, LLC.

"Every action done in company ought to be done with some sign of respect to those that are present."

George Washington, First President of the United States

It's a fact of life that many business deals and hiring interviews happen over meals. Knowing the dining rules no one ever told you could put dollars in your pocket. Dining etiquette can help seal a deal or make a positive impression that can land you a job offer or a better salary. With surprisingly little, easy-to-remember information, you can outclass your competition.

1 - Before the Meal

- Choose a restaurant that offers china plates, silverware, and cloth napkins. Style counts.
- If you are representing a business, you should comply with company policies on issues such as alcohol purchases.
- Order something that is easy to eat. Avoid foods like spaghetti, ribs, fried chicken, or spinach salad.

Know Your Place (Settings that is)

Think of the letters "B-M-W." They stand for:

- Bread – your bread plate is on your left.
- Meal – the main, center plate of the place setting.
- Water or wine – your glasses will be on the right. That includes your coffee cup and saucer.

Navigating your place setting requires some attention. Practice these tips before your meeting occurs. You'll feel much more comfortable and confident during the meal.

In an American-style place setting:

- Forks are on the left of the place setting. The outer fork may be smaller,
  as it is used for the salad course if it is
  served first.
- Use the utensils located farthest from
  the plate first. For example, the first
  fork you use will be in the left outer-
  most position of the place setting.
- Once used, the part of the utensil that
  was in your mouth never touches the
  table again. It must go on your plate,
  though the handle can extend off the
  plate. If it is a knife, the blade points
  downward with cutting edge facing
  the center of the plate.

American

Here is what the setting would look like
with all the possible pieces.

Place Setting Map

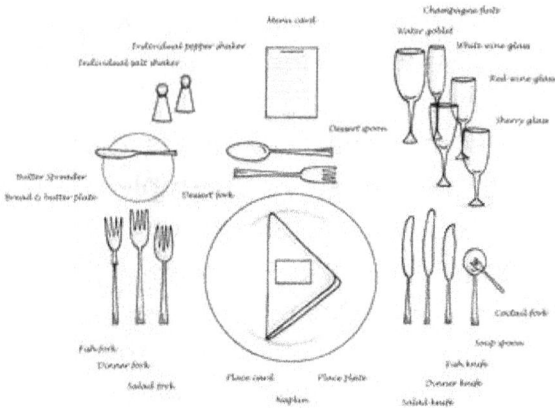

Champagne flute
Water goblet
White wine glass
Red wine glass
Sherry glass
Menu card
Individual pepper shaker
Individual salt shaker
Dessert spoon
Butter Spreader
Bread & butter plate
Dessert fork
Cocktail fork
Soup spoon
Fish fork
Dinner fork
Salad fork
Place card
Place plate
Fish knife
Dinner knife
Salad knife
Napkin

At the Table

- Wait for your host to indicate where you will sit.
- Once your host picks up her napkin, pick up your napkin quietly and fold it in half. Place the open end close to your waist with the folded end facing your knees.
- Order from the middle of the price range on the menu — not the most or least expensive items.

2 - During the Meal

Preparing to eat

- Eat with one hand and rest the other hand on the table at the wrist. Years ago, the rule was to keep one hand in your lap, but that is no longer regarded as mannerly.
- Taste your food before seasoning it with salt and pepper. If you must add salt, don't just grab it. If it is too far to reach, say, "Please pass the salt."
- Salt and pepper are passed together, like they're married, and passed to the right, counter-clockwise.

Biz Tip: All food passes to the right, counter-clockwise. Only exception is if someone is a few places away to the left.

Cutting your food

- Hold the food still with your fork and cut with a knife.
- Point the fork downward with your index finger on the back of the fork where it curves.
- Cut behind the backside of the tines of the fork, below where your index finger holding the fork is pointing.

- Cut no more than three pieces of food at a time (you are not a slicer 'n dicer).
- After cutting your food, place the knife on the plate and transfer your fork to your dominant hand (your right hand, if you are right-handed).

American Style
Resting

Mind your manners

- Take small bites and chew with your mouth closed.
- If you think something is caught in your teeth, simply say, "Excuse me," and go to the restroom where you can remove it privately.
- The same goes for blowing your nose or applying lipstick. Do it in the bathroom and not at the table.
- When you are leaving the table, fold your napkin and put it on the seat of your chair. This gesture tells others, "I will be back."

The Art of Conversation

It's not about the food. It's about the business conversation. Stay focused on business and stay off your cell phone.

Most meals begin with small talk.

- Safe topics for conversation are the weather, movies, sports, and books. Stay away from politics, religion, or sex, including inappropriate remarks or jokes.
- It may be during the main entrée that you begin discussing business. It just depends on how much time you have to meet.

Cells phones are more than user friendly. They're also germ friendly and typically carry more bacteria than the handle of a toilet.

- Keep your cell phone off the table, away from the food, turned to silent. Not vibrate . . . silent. Even better off.
- The only exception is if you have a relative in the hospital and are expecting an important call from the doctor.
- Alert your guest or host that you may get an important phone call during the meal.

- When such a call comes, say, "Excuse me," and step away from the table to a hallway or somewhere that you can have privacy. Not the restroom. Using a phone in a restroom violates the privacy of others. Besides, your phone doesn't need any more germs!

3 - Ending the Meal

Leaving a meal graciously is as important as eating it graciously. Knowing how to position your utensils demonstrates to both your guest and server you know business etiquette.

- Don't eat all your food. If you're still hungry, get something to eat on your way home.
- When finished, place your knife and fork on your plate diagonally, pointing from the 4 o'clock position toward the 10 o'clock position.
- Your knife's cutting edge should face toward 6 o'clock.
- Place your fork between the knife and the 6 o'clock position.
- Loosely fold your napkin and put it on the table to the left side of your place setting. This signals your server you are finished.

American Style
Finished

- Do not ask for a doggie bag. If your host insists on sending you home with a dessert or special item from the restaurant, accept it graciously.

After the Meal

The person who extended the invitation pays. The check is not a tug-of-war situation.

- If your host asks for the check, simply say, "Thank you."
- If you set up the meeting, you pay.

Biz Tip: If you are the host, arrive early and ask your server to hold the final check and you will pay after your guest leave. Provide your credit card if requested. This prevents the tug-of-war.

If you are representing a business, your company may have budget guidelines on tipping. Check them and comply with the policy. Be sure to give an appropriate tip. Remember, you are representing the company.

- Breakfast – 15%
- Lunch – 15 - 20%
- Dinner – 20 - 25%
- If your business lunch has lasted more than an hour, and your server could have served another group in that time, add another 10 percent to your tip.
- When possible, let your server know when you sit down that you expect your meeting to last a while and that you will "take care of" him or her.

4 - Powerful Finishes

Sometimes what you do after a business meal can be the deciding factor in getting the business deal.

- If your server was especially helpful, tell the restaurant manager. He/she will remember you the next time you come in and provide excellent service again.

- Write a note of thanks to your host within 24 hours after the business meal. This can be sent by email.
- A handwritten note on quality card stock is even better and leaves an impression of making an extra effort.
- Thank your business partner for their time and confirm again some main points from your meeting.

Chapter in Review

Your success begins before the meal. Choose a restaurant where you can conduct business in a quiet setting.

Think of your place setting as a B-M-W, which represents bread, meal, water or wine, the order of items from left to right.

After your meal, be sure to follow-through with a note of acknowledgement to your guest or host to thank them for their time.

THE TRANSITION TO POLISHED PROFESSIONAL

If you've taken the time to read through the entire book, you now know exactly what it takes to make the transition from college student, or entry-level worker, to the management team.

Over time, continue to think of your transition to new and different positions as having five phases: overcoming anxiety and fear, building self-confidence, becoming comfortable, developing self-esteem, and accelerating productivity and effectiveness.

Phase One is the state of the unknown where the new hire or newly promoted person usually starts. Not knowing or understanding the expectations of management, adjusting to a new group of team members, acclimating, to the corporate culture, taking on new responsibilities, and not knowing what they don't know but they need to know! This can create a level of anxiety and fear.

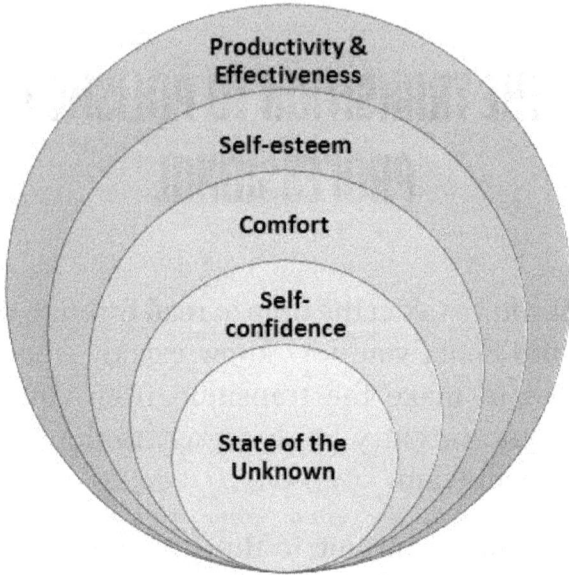

Productivity & Effectiveness

Self-esteem

Comfort

Self-confidence

State of the Unknown

Phase Two is when an individual identifies where they believe change needs to occur. It's being motivated to, and actually making changes that moves one towards building their self-confidence.

Phase Three is the comfort zone, where they become more at ease with their role and responsibilities within the department and organization. It's having confidence in one's own abilities. Anxiety and fear lessen, and self-confidence is evidenced through their performance and behavior.

Phase Four is self-esteem. It's being confident in one's own merit as an individual person, feeling that they can do things well and that people respect them.

Phase Five – enabled with self-esteem and confidence, the individual is catapulted into this phase, which results in an increase to their productivity, effectiveness and professionalism.

Good manners and professional behavior always trumps inappropriate conduct in any business, social, or personal situation. Be aware, motivated, and courageous to make the changes that are required for success.

I've tried to make this a book of helpful hints. Please use it as a guidebook and know that change doesn't happen overnight. My hope is from time to time you'll refer back to it as a tool to help you navigate your way through the phases of transition. From new hire to polished professional!

Wishing you the very best in your career.

YOU'LL WANT THESE!

We turned the best stuff from the book into quick-hitting cheat sheets – perfect for scrolling before your first day or a big meeting.

Scan the QR code or use the link – and thank yourself later!

https://bit.ly/c2c-cheat-sheets

ABOUT THE AUTHOR

Marla Harr is the owner and chief consultant for Business Etiquette International a company whose goal is to help others master the soft skills and techniques of business etiquette and protocol intelligence so they can achieve a competitive edge through the art of diplomacy. Certified and trained by the Protocol School of Washington® and backed by more than three decades of corporate management and educational development experience, she brings to her work a mixture of both entrepreneurial spirit and corporate professionalism.

After working in the corporate arena for several years, Marla started her own meeting and event company, experiencing first-hand the challenges of career transition and learning a new industry's culture and language. It was her mastery of these challenges and her love for helping others to excel professionally that led her to opening Business Etiquette International in 2007.

Marla is an adjunct faculty member at San Diego State University, former adjunct at Arizona State University, and California State University. She is an active member of Society for Human Resource Management (SHRM), Association for Talent Development (ADT), and National Speakers Association – Arizona chapter.

To see how you or your company might benefit from Marla's services, contact her at: mjharr1@cox.net. Or visit

https://3CManagementTraining.com

INDEX

O

Observation, **49, 51-52, 58**

P

Place setting, **126-127,132, 135**
Polite, **17, 22, 45,64,72, 77, 96**
Presentations, **103, 109**

R

Relationships, **6, 15, 22, 24, 42, 53, 72, 74, 82,
111-112, 115, 118, 121, 123**
Respect, **24, 37-40, 42, 45, 57, 61-64, 67, 77, 94,
108, 114-115, 122-123, 126, 139**

S

Self-control, **63, 77, 114**
Small talk, **21-22, 29**

T

Text message, **69**

U

Unspoken word, **6152**

V

Verbal, **16, 66, 75, 77-79, 96, 118**
Voice message, **1**

W

www.ingramcontent.com/pod-product-compliance
Lightning Source LLC
Chambersburg PA
CBHW070929210326
41520CB00021B/6866